Friends With Foe

Remember Me

Armanda Mota

BookLeaf Publishing

India | USA | UK

Made with ❤ on the BookLeaf Publishing Platform
www.bookleafpub.in
www.bookleafpub.com

Dedication

To the victims who have no voice and the ones who thought they had no choice. To the not being able to say good-bye and realizing that was the best part now. To childhood memories of friends, you dreamed of growing old with no matter the difference between us and never getting to see each other grow old. To the childhood friends reconnected after a tragedy and finding out your love is different and your time together a treasure. To the place I go while listening to music I still love today. To my old typewriter, paper, word processor, computer and now phone available for when my mind has lines of content to spill. To mental illness coming from all walks of life, when all you see is what shines on a television screen. To the undiagnosed, the medicated, the over medicated, under medicated and more. Dedicated the cases, some solved, some unsolved but are they really ever solved? Families still waiting for justice, answers, connections that may help them feel better, get closure, close a door? ***Meet me at the Station,*** *previously published in The Pawtucket Times, 2004. I am proposing the donate 1/2 of any proceeds I make from this publication to the care and maintenance at the Station Fire Park.*

Preface

Acknowledgements

1. Little did I Know

Little did I know
two months ago, you'd go
A full conversation never to exist
Little did I know
you wouldn't see the snow
and your name crossed off my Christmas List
Little did I know
you were there, then gone
Leaving me with no chance to tell you how I feel
Little did I know your approval of me was spoken
to only find later more about how you were so real
Four months was all I got
to see all of what you were to be
But he had better plans for you
he gave you wings and set you free
Saturday night, the last time I saw you
No chance for more
Your straightened hair, your smile
Your walk out the door
Little did I know

my feelings for you could grow
Four months is all I got
Enough time to feel, to love, to miss you a
lot……………………
-Armanda Mota

2. COPE

Why, we'll not yet know
Was it really your time to go?
Is there a plan we all hear about?
& are your wings pink? No doubt
Was the car you were in; the last ride you were to take?
And the phone call to people with good news; the last
you would make?
You got your drivers permit on that same day;
Suddenly I heard you were taken away
Up in flight to get you there
To make it better, to ease the fear
But loosing you was what was to be;
On Cross Road-a faded memory
The road so narrow & windy at times,
A replica of life with no rewinds
Of bad times, of the feelings that we felt
The trauma, no complete recovery we have dealt
No driving in your own car
No graduation day
August 14th, your "19th birthday"

Was I the one, who was supposed to be around?
For that hand to hold, for the moments I found
Had it not been you who changed my life.
Would I be happily married as his wife?
Why? We might never know
Was it really your time to go?
Was it really written this way, so that all
will join you in heaven some day?
I hope I feel the hand of grace
Take me to that special place.
To see your bubbly smiling face
I can only imagine
I can only hope
How your many loved ones cope
3 years are gone
Of a 16-year-old beauty queen,
An accident scene
Pink angel wings
A smile so true
Memories of you
Was it really your time to go?
We LOVE you more than you maybe already know
-Armanda Mota

3. Girlfriend

How can one move so quickly?

How can one soon forget?

-A human being's actions in life and not regret

How can one play the part and shortly close the door?

-Then open another memory, to selflessly want more

In life she didn't see, how priceless she was worth

A mother's first impression, the day she gave her birth

True colors they say, with more shades of gray

Reap what you sow, but girlfriend you already know...

That truly you are loved

and thought of still today

Even though life took our hands

and pulled the opposite way

You always seemed to still love me

even while words seemed to fall

You always would still call my name

with a smile, standing tall

If your heart and soul are aware

of what is being done

Please know that your memory is not a faded one

And although some may move so fast
Seem to forget and choose to run
Rest in peace-dear friend
Cuz we were the lucky ones!
-Armanda Mota

4. Her Voice

What you last heard was her **voice**
No sadness in her tone
Was she really leaving for Heaven?
Was she really all alone?
Did she know her last good-bye to you was not a happy
one?
Did she really want to say to you, my working day is
done?
Did you hear her voice and listen close to the words that
she did say?
Did she think her life on earth was over that Christmas
Eve day?
What you last heard was her **voice**
Not thinking it was your last
Given the chance again I'm sure
You'd go back to the past
Her **voice** is now heard within the world
A smile from ear to ear
A woman with child, a household name
Remembered with a tear

Her **voice** now lives within you
Her tears are strength inside
Don't give up on her memory
Let them be your guide
-Armanda Mota

5. Michael

Always a fan-not just now: Amanda

I know how you felt, I know some of what you went
through

But Michael, god up in heave will accept you for you

He will hold you and kiss you and erase what you feared

You will see there are truly people who cared

And although stories will haunt your name and follow
your

Every memory

Know that when I saw your face, it was sometimes me I
would see

There are no real judges here; no one can honestly say

I will keep your memory of what you were to me
anyway

Everything you touched, would shine in this little girl's
eyes

Your dance moves, your style, your wave good-byes

How I wanted that doll so bad, just to adore

But Michael it really doesn't matter anymore

For what I wish for you is more than any possession I

can find
Your walk alongside Jesus must be a special kind
I can only image your heart being so at ease
Your mind so content; your heart finally on your sleeve
Sad to see your life end this way; but it is not for anyone
of us to say
Sad to see your life the way it existed; no more tears, the
knots untwisted
Man in the Mirror, Thriller, Billie Jean and more
I guarantee you didn't have to knock on Heaven's door
You're rested now, no more can they criticize, this crazy
world, the sometimes lies
Of people unperfected and to themselves so untrue
The lives that they live; the things that they do
Your life so publicized; everything that you would say
Continues an open book and defines who you are today
Neverland never seemed so never or things that might
have gone wrong
MJ Rest in Peace; your life, your death, your last song
-Armanda Mota

6. PINK

Have you seen her smile,
and really engrave it in your mind?
Did you know that she would never return to a home
and find?
The family that truly loves her, while not knowing
what's in store
To lose a little girl, who once walked right through their
door
Those little things we take for granted, Hello and
Goodbye
Pink taken from your world, to only have to die
A senseless thing, numbness inside
Living a nightmare against a tide
Of fear parents feel
When our children step away
Telling them to be afraid of who may be out today
Time on the clock passes by, and slowly we must think
Where can they be? Prepare ribbons for Pink.
Pink, we see you
On a video one more time

So sad this Friday morning, to hear of this crime
The church that you lay beside
Not knowing what was in store
But God bought you to heaven, as you walked right out
that door
A child, so precious, so innocent and naïve
Taking the word of strangers, not knowing who to
believe
We can tell them, till we're blue
And our words may pass from their mind
But unfortunately, we live in a world where people are
not so kind
How can we protect our little Pink's world?
When there are Them's walking around
Do parents have to bury there's in order to make a little
sound?
Have you seen her smile
and erase it from your mind?
Knowing tomorrow they'll be a story of another kind
Where THEM's can take the hand, and lead them away
Where a child is overpowered, and has lived their last
day
And months turn into years
And parents are never the same
And people will soon forget an 11-year old's name
PINK to a list of pain, for years on end
A name not forgotten, to her family or friends

-Armanda Mota

13

7. That Book

My guide has rested me atlas
I am free to finally be
Please dry your eyes and smile
And live your life for me
I am no longer here for you to see
I have taken a hand to guide me
I did turn one last time to look
As you started to write in that book
I looked away, I had to go
I was promised to see you again
My time with you will never die
My heart, the love, my friend
-Armanda Mota

8. Tear

Who will cry when you can no longer bear?
Who will shed a final tear?
A preliminary hearing
A slap in the face
How can we imagine what's taking place?
A smile is now a memory
A face from sea to shining sea
An accused killer
With possibilities of being set free
Who will cry when your pain is so deep?
A bond so tight, no hug good-bye
A daughter doesn't want to see her mother cry
Trace over all your memories
Look for you will find
A tear of many shapes, a rare & special kind
Of a MOTHER laughing in the background
As tears roll down your face
Where she could be right now
In a very special place
Tears are for many reasons

And reasons are all too clear
A man accused of murder
His day is coming near
I can't believe the anger
I'm feeling deep inside
For a complete stranger
And a man who has lied
Why must we live this way?
How many times the pain?
All that pointing fingers
Looking for someone to blame
Hold on to that ride
Waves crashing on the sea
A thunder storm may come
Then the sun will shine for thee
Your tear will lead your heart
And inside it can no longer bear
The pain that keeps you going
The love and gentle care
Bring a tissue if you have to
Know that the world can see
Your heart will lead
his hands to another victory!
-Armanda Mota

9. Set of Wings

Sets of wings were waiting
Awarded one by one
Mom stood in line, behind her was her son
Approaching slowly she whispered
"I can't believe we're going to fly"
Then she noticed a different line....
This line had many people, with sad looks upon their
faces
Why two separate lines? Why two different places?
Overjoyed her turn was coming, a face she seen so clear
She turned to look again
What is he doing there?
Pretending he didn't know her, ashamed at what he had
done
Not knowing what his fate was, not recognizing his own
son
A tear fell slowly down her cheek, for now she can recall
That is the man, your father, the one who had it all
Turning away she wiped her face
Gaining composure for about to receive

A set of wings so she can fly in a place where she can
believe
Don't need that car to drive, she thought
It seemed he knew my fate
And know he stands in line, embarrassed...... well it's too
late
My home was once my temple
Instead, his choice was clear
To sell a place where I did live, but now I must live here
Now it's her turn
She is greeted with a smile
Check the list to see, but her name was not on file
This woman looks up at this mother, and sees a smile a
face cannot forget
Starts a conversation, she thinks they may have met
This mother tells her she's been waiting
In a line, so long she could see
The many wings in a pile
But could one be there for me?
The woman looks again
And then remembers that in another book
Is a list of lives who were innocently took
And there it was so big and bold
Two names of meaning, and stories that told
She them grabbed her hand and this little baby too
To take a different way
But this mother had to ask, and the woman had to say

That line is for the "pack of lies"
Heard so many times
And now each one must wait to pay
The ultimate fines
Instead of wings, a set of bricks
To remind them of the pain
Bestowed on many people
They must endure the same
The real judge is here waiting
There is no good reason why
But don't you even worry, it's here you learn to fly
How could he? She thought
Feeling deeply mad, she turned away once more
I now must look ahead and walk
Right through heaven's door
A special order of wings
A set for him and her dipped in gold for angels
Who lived their lives so pure
She tried them on
And they fit them to a tee
Looking up to Jesus, she asks
"What will become of me?"
Jesus responding:
Your son, he needs a mother
Your mother, she needs a prayer
Your husband, he needs a miracle
But the devil doesn't care

-Armanda Mota

10. Not Guilty

Not guilty, in the eyes of who?
Not truthful to those who loved you
Leaving ones to morn, no answers in sight
Not guilty, you say
So, stand up and fight
Not guilty, to whom?
Your lawyer and you
Not truthful to yourself, leaving one to see
The story that lives inside of you
You cannot set free
Not guilty, ok!
Who are we to say?
You're the one with the answers
On what happened that day
Not guilty, not funny!
For tears continue to fall
A young Mother-to-BE's memory
Lives inside of us all
Not guilty! Then what?
Does your story ring true?

Your pregnant wife waiting
For a baby in blue
Not guilty, then prove it
It sounds so damn fake
You're living a lie
For heaven's sake
Not guilty, obviously you don't care
You leave a mother in pain,
forever to bear
A family to face another day
A court room & cameras,
and still you say
Not guilty!!
-Armanda Mota

11. VLEE

If I

could

turn back time to see you
To laugh with you once more
I'd walk away from everything
and run right out this door
It seems we say that often
When things are much to late
Our lives seem to take over
this thing some call it -fate
Reality has not sunk in
As busy lives are in effect
Its then you finally feel
a piece of the missing wreck
A ship set off too soon
When most of us begin our start
A smile, a laugh broken
A past in pictures as art
Friends forever we used to say

No matter what we were glued
To say goodbye to the box
that your Heart is now tattooed
Breaks whenever I sit somber
and go back to those carefree
Yet sometimes troubled days
When you were there for me
I hear your voice so clearly
I hear you say my name
Your laugh I cannot forget
as the times, we overcame
The words we promised forgotten
While that road we chose hurried
Phone calls and visits
and now your presence buried
Much farther than you were before
and still, one seems to forget
Old friends are simply never
people we regret
They are always childhood memories
In all we can still recall
Without you I can't finish the words
To a forgotten story at all
-Armanda Mota

12. SoulsLikeU

2 years old,
2 short a life
Her mother looks on
Listening to words that cut like a knife
Who is lying now?
I don't understand
Is it hereditary? This bullshit
Coming out on the stand
We realize there is trauma,
That is so obvious to see
But there was this little girl
No longer to be
I would get my act together,
And give my best at what I could
Be the mother, grandmother etc...
I thought I should
For now she is no longer here
Not even able to defend
Whom she thought would protect her
The family she felt were friends

Yeah, her toys lay around the yard
And this swimming pool story
But really, does she now
receive eternal glory?
From our father, whom all say is good
But her grandfather lost in the woods
Miscommunication, abuse, little angel
So innocent, not knowing
The secrets of deception
Her family not showing
Why not take the stand-I would have
Fought till the end
I would have straightened out these loose pretends
If so true, they started this craziness in your soul
Open up a can and give them your all
Instead of sitting. sobbing and shaking your head
You are still alive, that little girl is dead
How fucked up to not scream and accuse these people
head on
After all the wrongs you made
Not even could you make one thing right
No fight!
They would lock me and medicate me some more
But never would I not speak to justify the score
Of someone so precious, so innocent and true
Little Angel

I hope Heaven is true for souls like you!
-Armanda Mota

13. Purple Hat Society

Purple Hat Society
We joked about that once
And why no more jokes
I still regret
You're time on earth, dear friend
Was too short, not yet
Done-underestimated
And your daughter-innocent
Your struggle, I was not a witness
But I hear of the fight-so militant
Thoughts of your unease
Bring me down to a place
Where many crawl out
And others still face
Down was the situation
But it seems up was your head
A shoulder to lean on
A hospital bed
I did not even visit
There was a disconnect

So close yet so far was you
A void left kept
Your plans left unfinished
Your responsibilities being done
Sometimes in life's woes
We reflect on the lucky ones
Not sure of what you're doing
Not sure if you see the past
At least I had the moments
A friendship, the longest last
Of when things seemed so difficult
And now knowing it was small
That time and thought now give us
A new reality-a wakeup call
-Armanda Mota

14. Angela

The one Angela had...
We seldom talk about the evil
The ones who walk by our side
As we let our children grow up
While under a mask, they hide
We seldom remind that evil
Lurking in our day to day
Can snatch you up in seconds
And simply drive away
We seldom think there's evil
Because who really wants to be dark?
Waking up to start the day
While carrying a little spark...
The one the Victim had...
The spark that lived inside her
A 19-year-old with a dream
Still evil walks among us
and shatters all that gleam
The one Angela had...
We seldom remember this evil

Even when confronted face to face
A courtroom of answers
While dressing an empty space
So seldom, we put our worries
in the hands of our God with LOVE
so often we forget how important
that message from above
The one Angela had...
Profoundly immoral and wicked
Is the adjective of this word
How one human beings' action
And the only voice that's heard
Let's remember the one Angela had...
-Armanda Mota

15. Hold On

Hold on to what is left of her
Don't let it slip away
For smiles are worth a dozen
As memories fade away
Hold on to things left by her
A card. A recipe, a funny inside joke
Watch videos of her spirit
And the words she may have spoke
Hold on too little stupid things
That some of us just toss
Its times like this you need
Anything to fill that loss
Hold on to the smile she always
Kept upon her face
I doubt she has changed much
Since leaving this place
Hold on to your pride
You wear it on your sleeve
The strength and courage
Give us hope to believe

Hold on to her happiness
Inside she probably already knew
Her life on earth was numbered
Or perhaps she had no clue
Hold tightly to what you love
And let go of some pain
You've given us a reason
You've given us a name
Of that a
Mother to be and her unborn son
The scar that it has left you
The terror that has been done.
-Armanda Mota

16. Meet me at the Station

Meet me at the Station, meet me on stage
Life is so unfair as we turn the next page
Not just another story book, not enough paper for them
to write
Loved ones lost in fire all before twelve o'clock midnight
Great White they call themselves, now Ty has sung them
to sleep
Little things left behind, is hardly enough to keep
One by one identified, a total nightmare to see, looking
to no one
How could this be?
Pointing fingers, searching for someone to blame
Waiting, not wanting to hear a familiar name
Sound proofing they say, so outsiders can't hear
Leaving people inside to face that fear
Pyrotechnic display on February 20,2003
Given wings and set those angels free
West Warwick's Station, what went wrong
Who finished hearing Great White's first song?
Can you imagine the screams, the fear and the cries?

Lift them up high into those blue skies
Killing nearly 100 and injuring roughly twice that
amount
Waiting to hear that final count...
They came from all around to watch this grand show
Some will watch from above to see their children grow
Many of the dead were found just inside the front door
Three minutes not enough, why didn't they get more?
Couldn't flee the fire in time to get out
Giving a chance, a benefit of the doubt
We must believe in heaven, what else must we do?
The golden gates have opened to let them all through
Much too soon, their lives were ending
Leaving too many hearts broken and bending
Meet me at the Station, meet me on stage
Don't be angry, don't be full of rage
I'm hearing songs in heaven, so peaceful and I feel free
My friends from Thursday night are here for me to see
I wasn't coming home, it was all a plan, and you'll
believe me when you see
My face, my wings, and my soul in heaven on the day
you come to me
Consumed with many memories, trying to forget
Taken for granted, life goes on, (Who said that)?
We can't go on, not yet!!!
If this is life, why so much pain
Is that supposed to be part of the game?

Sitting, crying and forever in shock
The memory still sits on some others block
No last good-bye, no kisses on the cheek
No more days to work, not one more week
Can't wait until Friday, why what's wrong with today
Almost one hundred die in just one day
Wipe all those tears; I stand by your side
I'll take you to heaven; I'll be your tour guide
The song kept on playing, I heard it loud and clear
They played the same song for us all; it was here that we
could hear
Meet me at the Station, meet me on stage
Here there's no minimum wage, I made my last deposit
No interest will I receive
One last thing I ask of you is "Please, please believe"
I took my last ride; the light has turned red
I can't feel any pain; I'm now lying in bed
The pace is really slow here; I'm no longer in a hurry
My scares are all healed, and I have not one worry
Meet me at the Station, meet me on stage
Life is so short as we turn the last page
No author's name was written, too many of them, no
chance
Grieve, but remember there is no last dance
The music is still playing; no tear is left in sight
I did say good-bye to you
On that Thursday night

You probably were busy or had another call
I felt no pain, when I took that fall
I closed my eyes; it was my time to go
Great White didn't have a chance to put on that show
Meet me at the Station; West Warwick, RI is where I'll be
I said good-bye on Thursday night
My wings have set me free!
In memory of all who died on February 20,2003 and for
all those still holding on!
-Armanda Mota

17. i hope you dance

I dreamt about you as you held me tight
Maybe consoling me as if to say "it's all right"
It felt so real as if it was really just you & me
But then I woke up suddenly.......
I thought about you more throughout my day
And wondered if I continued to sleep
Would you have had something to say?
Did you come around to remind me?
And not want me to forget
Of the memories we had, and the ones never met.
Were you there to wipe the tears still left to dry?
Please don't tell me you were saying goodbye
I can dream and wonder about this some more
Just know, I would never close that chapter, that door
Don't think for once I forget you and have nothing left
to say
Unfortunately, dreams don't always work that way
I hope you dance
-Armanda Mota

18. RW

Struggled through
life

And all around saw glamour & fame
Addiction, depression chooses no specific name
Funny, smart & talented
Looks like he had it all
A void that can't be filled
A last curtain call
How he made others laugh
While broken inside
Bringing joy to others
Must have lifted his pride
While he was falling....
Sadness consumes many
As they prepare to say good-bye
But a heart heavy
Will never really die
Free from what
He could not even explain

Cuz within it takes a hold of you
All you can describe is-pain
And not everyone understands
Not anyone can fix the broken
Nor will they comprehend his absence
Even after he had spoken
How one can finally give up...
And not because he didn't try
A smile starts to feel sore
A hug, it starts to sting
You mind was made up
Your life doesn't mean a thing
Selfish- I hear about this act
However, he gave, so much so long
Broken down and giving up
A man and his song
Don't lose your spark of madness
Rush hour really does move slow
For an illness laid in the background
For some in society who don't know
How one can finally give up
And not because they (he)
Didn't try
Perhaps.....
A smile starts to feel sore
A hug begins to sting
You feel heavy & tired

And no longer can you bring
Yourself to a new day.
-Armanda Mota

19. SMILE

Where did you go on December 24th, 2002?
Did anyone even see you?
A walk with the dog on Christmas Eve
What are the answers? Who to believe?
That smile on your face was ear to ear
Modesto, California waiting in fear
Eight months pregnant, it was baby and you
Hands reaching out, what can we do?
People sitting in wonder, watching TV
What is she doing? Where can she be?
The waiting just killing everyone inside
Oh, how you're loved, and oh how he lied
You couldn't be hard to miss
For you carried your baby around
Until that April unexpected day
When you and he were found
Your tears have all been dried now
For you can no longer see
The person who did this to you
Can live in misery

We've pointed our last finger
The answers are all too clear
What happened to the life
You three were supposed to share?
Could've been a man in black
Could've hit her like a heart attack
Instead, it was you, whose eyes were last seen
No one heard her cry, no one heard her scream
Picture perfect was her smile
Although pregnant you can see
Her smile was growing inside the womb
For a mother she was going to be
Hearts are left mending; tears are left to dry
Who was there to kiss her and say a last good-bye?
A bad nightmare for those who loved her
A smile that shined so bright
The lives of two were taken
No end to this dark, cold night
She taught some lessons
That we all could learn
Six by nine-foot cell for him
Now it's your turn
The answers soon will be clearer
Her name a memory
A smile in every picture
A saddened legacy
She waited by the gates of heaven

baby by her side
The Lord was approaching slowly
Arms were opened wide
His tears were falling for her
Memories of being crucified
It was he who sat beside her
When she was on that boat ride
Baby saying:
Our celebration party is waiting
A set of wings for mommy and I
They'll give us some leverage
And help us learn to fly
I'm glad I'm not alone here
My mommy by my side
He really didn't deserve her
Not even as his bride
All:
So now you face the penalty
And you'll pay on judgement day
That moment you took that smile
And threw their life away
-Armanda Mota

20. Christie Love

Living in your body
Not knowing what you felt
The many obstacles
The cards that you were dealt
You made it look so easy
There is no one here to blame
You need to rest, you did the best
The guilt, struggle and shame
Of no one
The chance missed
To take some pics
Thinking they'll be more
And yet we woke
With tears and choke
Till we see you again once more.....
Don't you dare let anything change you
If I did, you'd be upset
If only were only once
And fixed so we don't forget
I'd ask to hear your voice once more

If only was for sure

Christie Love

-Armanda Mota

21. 3 R's

3 Rr's in my childhood
Green house across the street
Memories I barely remember now
Didn't matter how we meet
Children not judging each other
Playing till the lights would shine
Even language at times, a struggle
But those three, they were mine
My friends, cuz I knew them
They'd be around sooner or later to visit
And when I'd check the windows
Frantic, not wanting to miss it
I remember being on the porch
And the old garage nearby
But summer wasn't the same
Without my polish friends and I
Pierogis always freshly made
Many family members to spare
I even met a new friend, Monika (RIP)
When I ran to visit there

Yes, we eventually caught up at school
Age and time, we sometimes fall
As we go about our business
And never make that call
Relying on Facebook to check up
Thirty years later, in a blink
Then you hear some news
With tears, you can't bear to think
What if? Why?
And what could I have done?
Many things come to your mind
When instead, you chose to do none
Regret that time is lost
And know you still have a chance
3 R's forever in my childhood
Rozann, I hope you dance
-Armanda Mota

9 789369 545278